WRITING ASEXUAL CHARACTERS

AN INCOMPLETE GUIDE

Salt & Sage Books

SALT & SAGE BOOKS

Cover designed by Blue Water Books

eBook ISBN 978-1-7349234-1-4

Paperback ISBN 978-1-7349234-3-8

Copyright © 2020

To the readers seeking to know their characters better, and in so doing, know the world better.

LETTERS FROM THE AUTHORS

Dear Reader,

Thank you for considering including an asexual character in your project! It's very easy for asexual individuals to feel that they are not complete. Sexuality is something that is so often painted as a feature that comes standard in all humans, something that everybody wants, thinks about, and is capable of.

I personally have often felt that I'll somehow never be a "real adult" if I don't hit certain sexual milestones; this fear is reinforced by a society that so often equates sex with worldliness and loss of virginity with entrance into adulthood. And as an asexual who is not aromantic, it's easy to feel that I'll never have enough to offer as a partner to make up for the inherent flaw of not offering sex—as if dating me is some sort of rip-off.

Here's the beautiful thing: any time I see myself reflected in media, all these insecurities start to melt off my shoulders. I'm reminded that people like me are complete, undamaged, and deserving of all the same things as our allosexual counterparts. I'm reminded that an interest in sex isn't what makes us human.

I hope this Guide will give you a beginning familiarity with the wide range of experiences that asexuality can stand for. As you'll learn, there are many ways to be asexual. We are all different, and all of our stories deserve representation.

Whatever asexual character has risen up in your mind and asked you to share their voice with the world, please take the time to listen deeply. Happy writing!

Tova

WHY THIS BOOK?

Dear Reader,

Welcome to the first of Salt & Sage Books' Incomplete Guide series. We're glad to have you here!

Do you remember the first time you read a book and thought, "Ah! That's me!"? That ringing inside of being seen?

I do. As a child, I was obsessed with a Cinderella book. Cinderella was white, blond, and female, just like me. I was probably two.

As we interview for Salt & Sage, we ask, "When have you felt seen?" The answers we've heard from our incredible editors & readers have been inspiring and heartbreaking. Some of them have been avid readers their whole lives, but have yet to read about someone who looks like them, feels like them, talks like them.

That's where you come in, dear author, ready to write those characters, ready to look beyond stereotypes, ready to write whole people.

Salt & Sage is all about quality editing with kindness—and kindness isn't just an encouraging tone in an edit letter or complimentary in-line notes. Kindness is helping authors like you (like me!) who want to do better and be better, but aren't sure where to start. That meant providing a level of sensitivity reading beyond a basic rubber stamp of yes/no.

As sensitivity reads flowed in and out, I noticed a pattern: the same concerns were appearing again and again in the letters from our asexual readers. I saw the same pattern from our trans readers. Once I noticed it, the pattern showed up everywhere: our sensitivity readers were regularly rehashing the same concerns related to their identities.

That got me thinking—if our authors were consistently having the same issues, could we help in a more targeted way? And what about the authors for whom a sensitivity read is too expensive?

The more I thought about it, the more I liked the idea. I've talked to lots of people in the writing world about writing diversely, and the same thing stops nearly all of them: fear. They don't know where to start. They aren't sure that their Googled information is accurate. They don't know anyone who they can ask, or they are too nervous to ask.

After lots of brainstorming about the best way to provide this information, the Incomplete Guides were born. You're currently reading our *Incomplete Guide to Writing Asexual Characters*. This was written entirely by our asexual readers and editors. They've addressed the most common areas of concern that pop up in their sensitivity reading. You'll see sections where they write from their own point of view, and where they share things that are person.

We are grateful to them for their vulnerability and openness within this *Guide*.

As you read this, you might find yourself feeling uncomfortable. That's okay. Take a deep breath and lean into the discomfort. Remember that unlearning (and re-learning) requires concerted effort and real intention.

Of course, even though this was written and edited by multiple asexual editors, we called the guide *incomplete* for a reason—it's not a blank check, nor is it a rubber stamp. Even if you address everything in this guide, you should still seek input from at least one member of the community you're writing about.

Salt & Sage Books has sensitivity readers on staff. Many authors also have success posting about their specific needs on Twitter's writing hashtags. Be sure to pay your readers for their labor. Listen carefully to their feedback, and you will most certainly write a better book.

We hope that *The Incomplete Guide to Writing Asexual Characters* will be a helpful resource as you write diversely. We invite you to step inside the viewpoint of our editors and experience a deeper, more impactful form of researching. We hope that will help you confront your own biases when writing asexual characters.

Mostly, we hope that you will continue to create thoughtful, nuanced asexual characters. We hope that you will be part of the movement to create more diverse books. It's critical work. It's occasionally difficult. It's deeply worth the effort.

May you write books that help people feel seen.

Erin Olds (she/her)

CEO, Salt & Sage Books

INTRO TO ASEXUALITY

So what exactly is asexuality? Where does it fit along the LGBTQIA+ spectrum? Is it an orientation or something else? How do you write a character who is asexual? Let's talk about the basics...

Asexuality is a sexual orientation that entails a lack of sexual attraction.

Asexuality is about attraction, not action: some people include other actions, attitudes, and beliefs in how they conceptualize their asexuality, but nothing is inherent in asexuality except for a lack of attraction.

Asexuality, simply put, is the lack of sexual attraction. This is both the most important as well as the determining factor in asexuality. Some asexuals, or aces for short, enjoy the act of sex itself. Others may not care for sex but are not put off by the idea. Some are even repulsed by the act, doing their best to stay as far away from anything referencing sex as possible. Whether or not they enjoy the act itself, the only descriptor of an ace that matters is that they are not sexually attracted to another human being.

It may help to think of it this way: a heterosexual person would be able to see a member of the opposite sex, find them attractive, and perhaps entertain the thought of a sexual interaction with that person. Homosexual people could see a member of the same sex and have a similar thought process: they could think the person attractive, enjoy their company, and want to take specifically that person to their bedroom. That could happen with two sexes for bisexual people, anyone at all with pansexual people, or only good friends for demisexual people.

Asexuals, then, simply are not sexually attracted to anyone. An ace might be able to find someone pleasing to look at, but a good-looking person doesn't inspire thoughts of a sexual nature about them.

To illustrate this idea, I am not the biggest fan of red velvet cake. I can see a beautifully decorated red velvet cake and absolutely love the way it's shaped, colored, designed, and frosted.

However, while several people might see that cake and instantly crave dessert, I would look at the cake, think that it's rather nice, and be on my way, simply because I don't care for a slice of red velvet cake. It doesn't matter how tasty it is to those around me, it just doesn't appeal to me.

Some people like me might want cake and not care at all how the cake is decorated or how it tastes, though they might not necessarily crave it. Others like me can't even stand the smell of cake batter and have to leave the bakery as soon as they can. But none of these people would see the cake, admire its beauty, and think, "Man, I really want a slice of that specific cake."

You may wonder, "Wait, how can someone who's asexual find someone good-looking? Wouldn't that mean that they are attracted to them?"

That's a good question, but attraction isn't quite that simple. To truly understand asexuality you need to understand that there are multiple types of attraction. The five types of attraction are sexual attraction, romantic attraction, physical attraction, emotional attraction, and aesthetic attraction.

Sexual attraction, of course, is the attraction that makes a person want sex with the person they're attracted to. Romantic attraction, while often accompanied by sexual attraction, is different in that romantic attraction is based solely on a desire to be in a long-term relation-ship with the person they're attracted to. The feeling of romantic attraction is a lot stronger than regular friendship and will often lead to wanting to do romantic things with their part-ner. What these romantic things are depends on the people involved, but as a general rule, if someone wants to do things that make them feel close to that person in more than a platonic or familial manner, then it's likely romantic attrac-tion pulling the strings.

Physical attraction is a desire for non-sexual touch from another person, such as hugs, high fives, or fist bumps. Emotional attraction is a desire to be emotionally open and connected with that person, whether they be friend, family, or partner. Lastly, aesthetic attraction is nothing more than thinking the individual looks good.

This actually allows for a lot of variety in writing an asexual character. You *could* write an asexual character who only interacts with people cordially and is generally emotionally closed off, or who gets anxious from the mere prospect of a relationship, but this would be incomplete. You could just as easily write an asexual character who loves cuddles, wears their heart on their sleeve, notices every good-looking stranger they pass by, and yearns for their other half. Asexual people are just as diverse as people of any orientation, so feel free to write them as such.

CHARACTER & STORY IMPLICATIONS:

An asexual character in your story will probably not be obviously asexual to the other characters around them. Your character could easily pass as another orientation due to their romantic attraction, if they experience it.

This could prove problematic to your character if they find themselves in a romantic relationship where their partner wants to take things further and your character doesn't want to. Such situations could lead to an outright denial of your character's sexuality.

They also lead to false and harmful accusations, such as infidelity, dishonesty about their commitment, doubts about mental stability, or even claims that the partner is being used to hide your character's true orientation, especially if your character has previously chosen to be sexual with their partner.

In some drastic cases, your character could even be abused due to their asexuality, although if they are, be sure to handle the subject carefully, as the topic is distressing and even traumatic to some individuals.

If your character is alive during a time when persecuting the LGBTQ+ community is common, then they might experience some shame, ridicule, or outright harassment, especially if your character doesn't appear to show interest in heteronormative relationships. They could be incorrectly outed as gay or lesbian and persecuted for it, under the false assumption that if someone isn't dating as a straight person, then they must secretly harbor attraction to others of the same sex.

If your character is in a society that is generally more accepting of other orientations, then they might be accepted as asexual, but they could just as easily be told that they're in denial about their attraction.

Regardless of when your character is alive, they've probably been told that their identity isn't real, that they just haven't found the right person yet, or that they're just ashamed of the way they feel.

2

UNCERTAINTY AND IDENTIFYING
AS ASEXUAL

A s with any orientation, identifying as asexual can be a quick and certain process, or one that involves a lot of uncertainty and questioning. This is complicated by the fact that it can be harder to identify by virtue of being a *lack* of attraction. This can cause uncertainty in the sense that it is easier to notice an attraction to someone else than the absence of attraction.

It can also cause uncertainty in the sense that it can be difficult to sort out the type of attraction one is feeling, and whether it is aesthetic (wanting to look at someone), sensual (wanting to be close to someone), platonic, romantic, or sexual. When someone is uncertain whether they are asexual, they might be wrestling with some of that uncertainty—do I want to be her friend, or do I want to date her?

Gender

This can be complicated by uncertainty around gender identity. There is precious little scientific research on asexuals or trans people, let alone both, but there is anecdata aplenty of people trying to figure out if their feelings towards someone are wanting to have sex with them, wanting to be friends with them, or wanting to be them.

Traditional gender roles can also play a role. Within a society that pushes the narrative that all men want sex, and that heterosexuality in particular is an inextricable part of being a man, the idea of not experiencing sexual attraction can be internally difficult to consider, and be shut down hard if raised with others. The flip side of that narrative impacts women raised with the idea of strong sex-positivity (everyone has sex and wants sex!), and women raised with the idea that it's both natural and good for women not to want sex, but simply put up with it for the sake of a partner. All of these can lead to people arriving well into adulthood before realizing that their experience doesn't fit with their "normal" peers.

Compulsory heterosexuality, as well as compulsory sexuality as a whole, can play a role here. Surrounding people with the narrative that all people are heterosexuality from infancy onwards can lead people to believe that that must be what they are experiencing, even when it very much is not.

For example, a lesbian inundated with societal messaging on heterosexuality might consequently believe that she is heterosexual, and not conceive of the possibility of sexual or romantic attraction to women on her part. As such, her feelings towards another girl must be platonic attraction, while her feelings towards another boy must be sexual attraction, with the different feelings impossible to unravel until she adds the possibility of sexual and/or romantic attraction to women to her mental framework.

Similarly, an asexual woman inundated with societal messaging of sexuality might consequently believe that they experience sexual attraction, and that said attraction is heterosexual.

This can also lead some asexuals to identify as pansexual or bisexual before identifying as asexual; if you feel the same attraction towards women as you feel towards men, and society says that you must be attracted to one, the other, or both, it must be both. Right? Finding out that not feeling sexual attraction is a possibility can be instrumental in people evaluating their own feelings and experiences.

Of course, there are people who figure out on their own that it's possible to feel no sexual attraction; but realizing in isolation that you do not feel sexual attraction in a world where it seems everyone must feel sexual attraction can make people feel as though there is something wrong with them.

Now let's combine our examples and consider an asexual lesbian raised in compulsory sexuality and compulsory heterosexuality, who figures out that she is romantically but not sexually attracted to women. This requires moving past the idea that she must be heterosexual *and* detangling romantic and sexual attraction. Depending on herself and her social environment, it could be a quick process or it could be a very long one.

All of this assumes that there is a right answer at which to arrive. There is not necessarily a finish line to this uncertainty, and to sexual identification in general. Someone might never be sure for themselves whether they are "really" asexual or demisexual, and this may be distressing or fine or completely irrelevant to their larger view of their identity. Even arriving at certainty is not necessarily the end; identifying as asexual does not have to be a final destination of orientation.

Sexual identity labels are meant to fit people, not the other way around. A person can identify as asexual, realize that they were mistaken, and not have been in the wrong.

I very much do not speak for all of us when I say that I believe that a person can identify as asexual and later identify as something else because their underlying sexual orientation has changed, not just the label—and what matters in that situation is how they themselves feel. This is controversial, even within the asexual community.

Much of the scholarship (and societal convention) around sexual orientations relies on the orientation being fixed in order to count as such, and for a lot of sexual minorities, the idea that orientation is both innate and unchanging is a fundamental component of identity.

Meanwhile, people who hold that their identity in relation to asexuality/allosexuality has changed after trauma, medical transition, or another life event are part of our communities too. For them, the idea that it can shift, that you can have been demisexual and now be asexual and both be true is also a fundamental component of identity. There is no arbitrator of sexuality who can declare who is right.

This raises the question: is it ok to write a character who thinks that they are asexual, but turns out to actually be allosexual? What about a character who *is* asexual at one point, but eventually is not?

This is a very fraught issue. On the one hand, a lot of allosexuals, including medical and mental health professionals, believe that asexuality isn't real and that someone who identifies as asexual must be incorrect, lying, mentally or physically ill, celibate but still attracted, and/or traumatized.

If it is real, it is a phase; something to be grown out of and moved on from, something that can be fixed through therapy or medication, corrective rape or the power of a loving relationship.

In this context of invalidation, there are very negative connotations around a character who thinks they are but turns out not to be, as that narrative reinforces the idea that all asexual people are that way.

Writing a story with this arc runs the risk of reminding asexual readers of traumatic invalidating experiences, and of telling allosexual readers that creating those traumatic experiences is not just ok but encouraged.

But. All of the above being said, people can be themselves uncertain about whether they are asexual or traumatized or repressed or have no libido, and it's important that people can be allowed to question their sexuality regardless of what the answer ends up being. Their experiences matter, and they deserve representation too.

Here is a popular comic by and for questioning aros and aces on the subject.[1]

***

Character & Story Implications

An asexual character could know their identity from the beginning of the story; they could start the story trying to figure it out and end it still trying.

Other aspects of your asexual character's identity will play a role here, both in terms of the external resources to know that asexuality exists, and the internal realization that it applies to them: are they (or did they grow up in) a highly allo- and/or heteronormative environment? Are they particularly introspective and self aware? Do they have a romantic orientation that might impact their realization?

Whatever you do in your writing, please just remember that asexuals of both camps could read it, care about it, and be hurt by it, and be kind in your approach.

———————————————

1. https://www.reddit.com/r/asexuality/comments/ dfb8a8/honestly_this_comic_is_great_for_explaining_s ome/

3

ARE ASEXUALS PART OF THE LGBTQIA+/QUEER COMMUNITY?

While you're writing your character, you may wonder whether or not they count as members of the LGBTQ+ community. After all, they have their own pride flag, but they aren't necessarily attracted to others of the same sex, romantically or otherwise. If you're left scratching your head on whether they belong in the queer community or if they should stay in their own asexual lane, then this next section is for you.

Now, before I get into the controversy in the LGBTQ+ community about asexuals, let me set one thing straight: they unquestionably are members of the community *if they choose to be.* What I mean by that, I'll explain here in a bit.

The most accepting acronym that sees common use is LGBTQIA+, which covers Lesbian, Gay, Bisexual, Transgender, Queer/Questioning, Intersex, and Asexual/Aromantic/Agender individuals, with the plus sign covering other identities not displayed in the acronym. The reason for this inclusion is that asexuals are, by definition, not heterosexual. Even if they're heteroromantic asexual, they still don't fit the traditional cisgender, heteroromantic, and heterosexual model, or cishet model, and consequentially are not straight. Since anyone who is not straight is automatically LGBTQ+, then it stands to reason that asexuals must also fit in the community if they so choose.

However, there are a myriad of reasons they may not choose to identify with the community.[1]

One of these reasons is that most of the community is inherently about either sexual attraction (as is the case of lesbians, gay men, bisexual people, and pansexual people) or sexual identification (as is the case of transgender, intersex, genderfluid, and nonbinary people, to name a few). Some asexuals may feel uncomfortable with being in a community so focused on sex, and so they respectfully decline membership in the community while still respecting them. The community is still open to them, but they have chosen not to be associated with them, which is a perfectly valid choice.

Another, more upsetting reason is that some members of the LGBTQIA+ community, called "exclusionists," do not see asexuals as worthy of community acceptance. Common reasons among exclusionists include the belief that asexuality isn't real, the belief that asexuals are mentally ill and shouldn't tarnish what the group stands for, or even that asexuals haven't been oppressed enough to deserve the resources and respect the LGBTQIA+ community has to offer. This is not only a cruel and invalidating form of gatekeeping, it's also factually inaccurate.

While homosexual people have certainly suffered more violent and extreme prejudice than any asexual is likely to experience, it is incorrect to say that they aren't discriminated against.

For example, in 2019, in a survey of 1,119 people, 53% said they could explain asexuality, but 75% of those people described it as little to no libido and not a valid orientation.

This belief that asexual people must have something wrong with them is widespread, which leads to a fear of coming out in asexual people. In a 2017 survey led by the government of the United Kingdom, of all cisgender respondents, asexuals are tied with pansexuals for lowest average life satisfaction, are the least comfortable cisgender LGTBQIA+ group in the UK, and are the least open cisgender group about their sexuality for fear of experiencing negative reactions.

In addition, in two separate studies, most notable being the "Prejudice Against 'Group X' (Asexuals)," it was found that between heterosexuals, homosexuals, bisexuals, and asexuals, asexuals are viewed in the most negative light and are more dehumanized than the other three groups, being compared to robots or animals instead of actual people. There are even strong beliefs that asexual people are sick and must either be "cured" by doctor visits or raped so that they can "learn to enjoy" sex. These beliefs are incredibly harmful to asexual people and ought to be removed from our society.

Given that asexual people do not fit the "straight" model and have certainly experienced prejudice and harm, I'd say that asexuals have earned their place in any open LGBTQIA+ community, which, to be honest, shouldn't ever have been in doubt in the first place.

The last thing to mention regarding the inclusion of asexuals in the LGBTQIA+ community is dispute over what the letter "A" stands for: it stands for asexual.

Some people claim that the "A" stands for "allies," and is included to celebrate the bravery of straight allies for standing with their LGBTQ friends.

While this might have been the case and we appreciate allies and their efforts, it is both ace erasure and insensitive to other LGBTQIA+ people to claim a space in the community, simply because they aren't LGBTQIA+ and will not experience as much persecution from supporting them as they ever would from being one of them.

***

CHARACTER & STORY IMPLICATIONS

Your character may likely experience discrimination due to their asexuality, both by cishet people and other LGBTQ folks. They may likely not be accepted in queer communities online due to the prejudice of exclusionists. Due to this, your character may choose not to identify with the LGBTQ community and might even harbor some resentment for them, choosing instead to stick with asexual-only groups and forums. On the flip side, they could potentially be part of an accepting group and embrace their identity as queer, and never once feel excluded. Nonetheless, if you're writing an asexual character in the modern world, they have almost certainly at least perused these online discussion boards and websites, so be prepared to factor that in if it comes up.

Regardless of whether or not your character is discriminated against, remember that the choice of whether or not to identify as LGBTQ is still up to them, not the rest of the world. Your character could join because they are asexual, or they could join because they are transgender or homo/bi/panromantic and never once mention their asexuality. How they identify is up to them, and while most asexuals will choose to identify because of their asexuality, that does not have to be the case for your character.

---

1. https://www.huffpost.com/entry/lgbt-asexual_n_3385530?1371820877

4

TROPES: ASEXUALITY AS CELIBACY

There are a couple tropes that capitalize on the idea that all asexuals are merely celibate: Hiding Behind Asexuality Trope and the Intellectual Trope.

HIDING BEHIND ASEXUALITY TROPE

Characters who fall into this trope are actually allosexual people who are just afraid of actually having sex.

These characters are typically socially awkward virgins who are incapable of making a move due to some temporary condition, such as shyness, as demonstrated in *The Olivia Experiment*[1], or a medical condition, such as in *House*, S8E09, "Better Half."

. . .

THE INTELLECTUAL

This character appears asexual but is only celibate so that they aren't distracted from intellectual pursuits.

A classic example of this trope is the titular character of **BBC**'s *Sherlock*.

These tropes can overlap with asexuality, with some asexual characters being nothing more than celibate but awkward geniuses who are terrified of sexual interactions, but don't confuse these tropes with actual asexuality.

PICTURE THIS: SOMEONE BORN INTO A RELIGIOUS family decides that they are not going to marry, and instead will devote their life to their deity or an order within their religion.

In high school, they find someone that they find attractive and want to take to the upcoming dance, but they refrain from doing so in order to prevent themselves from entering a relationship that they'll have to end.

In university, they are tempted by the prospect of a one-night stand, but ultimately decide that their choice to live sexless is more important.

Eventually, when most of their peers are married or otherwise committed and their family expects them to do the same, they instead cut themselves off from the dating world so they aren't distracted from their goal.

Compare this to another person, who has an innate curiosity for all sorts of experiences.

They went on several dates in high school and ended up in a relationship that lasted for a few years.

In university, they got curious, and decided to try hooking up with different people, only to come away from those experiences confused and somewhat unenthused.

When most of their peers are in relationships, monogamous, polyamorous, or otherwise, they finally end up in a marriage of their own that satisfies their romantic needs while never once initiating sex, though they might engage in it to please their partner.

It's pretty hard to confuse these two people, right? One obviously wants a sexual relation-ship, but refrains because they chose not to either marry or have sex. The other has no desire for a sexual relationship but may engage in sex anyway with the person they're married to.

This story of two people clearly illustrates the difference between two entirely different topics that people may find similar or confusing: the first character is celibate, whereas the other person is asexual.

So, what's the big difference? Let's start with celibacy.

Celibacy is the practice of abstaining from marriage and sexual actions. Anyone can be celibate, as the only requirement is that you have to choose not to marry or have sex. Celibacy is generally practiced within the context of religion, most notably Catholic monks and nuns, but can be practiced for any reason by anyone from atheists to Wiccans. The ultimate factor in celibacy is that it's a choice. It's voluntary. It's not something that anyone is born with. It can be entered and exited at will. Above all, it's a personal decision that may or may not be permanent.

Compare this to asexuality. Asexuality isn't a choice, but instead a lifelong sexuality. Anyone can be asexual, as the only requirement is to experience little to no sexual attraction. However, it is not a practice. If you are born asexual, you can't change that. The most defining factor is that it's a key part of someone that cannot be taken away by any means, even by the ace themselves.

There can be a lot of overlap between celibate people and aces, as asexuals often choose to live celibate lives for a number of reasons, including sex-repulsion, the expectation of sex in marriage, or just plain lack of interest.

However, as we've mentioned in earlier sections, asexuals can and sometimes do have sex. They can enjoy the act and might even have a high libido, but they just aren't sexually attracted to the people they are with. Due to the stereotype of the sex-repulsed asexual, though, it can be easy to believe that an asexual is just an allo-sexual who is really good at celibacy, or that asexual people can only be celibate and nothing else. Fortunately, nothing can be further from the truth.

Be careful not to confuse these tropes with actual asexuality, as true asexuals don't just become that way after being celibate. Learning to work around these tropes will help you to write more realistic, believable asexual people.

CHARACTER & STORY IMPLICATIONS

Just as this trope is commonly believed in real life, the characters in your story may likely believe the same things about your asexual character. Here are a few things to consider when you are writing your character and the characters around them:

You can still write a celibate ace, and it can still be realistic. Remember that your character is probably going to run into people who will either guess that they're asexual, which they are, or that they're hyper-religious, which they might or might not be. In either case, this can potentially cause problems for your character, as aces and/or a specific religion could carry a bad connotation in the context of your story.

Conversely, your character might be more open about being ace, only for others to attempt to invalidate that claim and try to make them "lighten up" a bit. This could prove equally problematic for your character, especially if other characters attempt to force them to "accept" a sexuality that they do not have. Of course, this can be played as lightly as a bit of comedy if you're careful, but most likely it's going to prove to be antagonistic toward your character.

Remember that despite the stereotypes that some people may try to put forth, an asexual character is not secretly just really good at being celibate. If your character is depicted as asexual until it's revealed that they secretly aren't, then make sure that there is a meaningful, plot-driven reason for them to be in the closet. Under NO circumstances should it be suggested in a positive light that all aces are nothing more than celibate liars. That is a harmful stereotype that continues to hurt real aces everywhere and there is no need to contribute to it.

---

1. https://www.bitchmedia.org/post/were-not-broken-asexual-characters-in-pop-culture

5

TROPES: ASEXUALITY AS
DESEXUALIZATION

There is very little awareness of asexuality as an actual sexual identity, which translates into very little intentional representation of asexual people. Absent intentional efforts to write asexual characters, many of the asexual characters that are created are not so much asexual as desexualized. This practice of stripping characters of their sexuality is general done to reinforce another segment of their character—to illustrate the extent to which they are childish, frigid, cruel, or inhuman.

There are several different iterations of these tropes. While fragmented at first glance, they are united in their use of desexualization as a form of denying agency to the given character. We will discuss the Eternal Child Trope, the Disabled or Sick Trope, the Ice Queen or the Frigid Woman Trope, and then look at intersectional problems of desexualization that span all of these tropes.

All of these tropes reinforce the real life desexualization of minority groups as a method of dehumanizing and denying agency to real people.

The Eternal Child Trope

In this trope, the asexual character is mentally younger or more pure/naïve than their allosexual characters by dint of their asexuality. This tends to be a character who never thinks about, has no interest in, and has never had sex.

Just like autistic and disabled people who battle the same infantilization stereotype, an asexual adult is an adult.[1]

The Disabled or Sick Trope

In which asexuality is conflated with low sex drive, and the asexual character has a low sex drive as a symptom or side effect. In this trope, it is presented as something that can and should be fixed. If the character identifies as asexual, they aren't *really* asexual, they just don't realize that they're sick.[2]

COMMON TROPE: THE ICE QUEEN, OR THE Frigid Woman

In which the asexual character is a socially distant, intimidating, or cruel woman. Frequently a, if not the main, villain, this character is a bad person who is bad in part because of refusing men—including sexually. This plays into larger misogynist tropes.[34]

INTERSECTIONAL DESEXUALIZATION

Asexual people are, of course, not the only marginalized group that is desexualized as a means of infantilization. For example, disabled people are frequently desexualized as a means of infantilization.

MLM ("man loving man") and WLW ("woman loving woman") also face desexualization (in addition to fetishization) as ways to make them seem less threatening to cis straight people.

People of color are desexualized as part of dehumanization.

Importantly, people in all of these communities can be asexual, and face backlash for "contributing" to desexualization through their identity, their choice to be out about it, and/or their existence.

As such, this very much not meant to tell you not write asexual characters who are otherwise marginalized—please, please do so because we need those stories on multiple levels.

It instead means to be conscious of the extra layer of context, so that when you write your story you avoid reinforcing those narratives and both reinforce and help build the supply of positive representation for all asexuals!

A helpful framework to separate out desexualization versus asexuality in real life is to remember that asexuality is an aspect of the person, whereas desexualization is done to the person.

This is, on the face of it, impossible to do in writing: although it certainly seems sometimes that characters have a mind of their own, you are by definition "doing to" characters.

A useful way to use that framework when writing is to consider whether it is playing a role of desexualization within the narrative. Is their asexuality used to reinforce anything else about them as a character—their personality, their health, their humanity, the threat they pose to other characters, etc?

If so, it's worth considering how to get that other aspect across without relying on asexuality to do so.

CHARACTER & STORY IMPLICATIONS

Consider whether your representation is incidental *desexualization* rather than intentional and affirmative *asexualization.*

Consider the reinforcement test from above; is their asexuality being used to reinforce another aspect of their identity?

Note that in considering this framework, it is one thing to have their asexuality used to reinforce other aspects of their identity by the narrative, and quite another to have it be interpreted as reinforcing other aspects of their identity by another character. One tells us about the other character(s); the other tells us something about asexuality as a whole.

As you evaluate potential tropes and pitfalls, consider whether your story is enforcing the first or the second.

---

1. https://slate.com/human-interest/2018/10/asexuality-awareness-week-infantilization-phase.html
2. https://www.salon.com/control/2012/01/31/house_gets_asexuality_wrong/
3. https://www.theatlantic.com/international/archive/2012/07/10-tropes-about-women-women-should-stop-laughing-about/325782/
4. Although not explicitly related to asexuality, the tropes discussed here frequently cross over with desexualization: https://tvtropes.org/pmwiki/pmwiki.php/Main/IceQueen

6

TROPES: ASEXUALITY AS DEHUMANIZATION

I'm gonna be honest with you here, this last trope is probably the most hurtful thing for any asexual to have to digest.

We've been told we're broken or immature, and that hurt a lot, in part because we've often thought that same thing ourselves. We've been told that we're just too scared for sex, so when we can't find any fear within ourselves, we question if maybe we are just suppressing trauma.

But when we are told that we are simply inhuman, and that to be sexless is to be feared and fought against, it makes a really deep cut, for what are we, if not human?

Let's discuss the three sub-tropes of the Dehumanized Asexual Trope: the Literally Inhuman

Asexual Trope, the Cold Hearted Asexual Trope, and the Death-Adjascent Asexual Trope.

The Literally Inhuman Asexual

This isn't inherently a bad trope, but it's probably the most common of the dehumanization tropes. Usually, if there's an asexual character in a story, it's probably a robot, such as Data from *Star Trek: TNG* or any of the droids from the *Star Wars* series. If not a robot, then the character could likely be an alien, such as Odo from *Star Trek: Deep Space Nine*. [1]

In many of these instances, the character is nothing more than a vessel to talk about what it means to be truly human and is often given asexuality as another "inhuman" trait. Sure, it's okay to have asexual characters who aren't human, but it begins to be problematic when said character's inhumanity is partly defined by their asexuality.

The Cold-Hearted Asexual

The trope of the Cold-Hearted Asexual is an extension of the Inhuman Asexual trope. Often used to prove a character's evil nature, this trope mixes traits like sociopathy, psychopathy, and misanthropy with asexuality in order to solidify a villain as heartless.

Most notable is Lord Voldemort from the *Harry Potter* series who is canonically aroace. Other prominent and incredibly evil characters also fit this trait. The Joker in the *Batman* comics only ever uses sex in the context of an evil, twisted act, while Light Yagami in *Death Note* only uses the promise of a relationship to cover his tracks and kill as many people as he can.

In all cases, they are portrayed as asexual in order to emphasize their horrendous qualities. Seeing as most asexual people and even most aromantic people are not like this, but media continues to portray them as such, this trope is rather damaging to the view that the world tends to hold about aces in general.

THE DEATH-ADJASCENT ASEXUAL

The last of the three examples of the dehumanized ace is that of the Death-Adjacent Asexual.[2]

This trope is a means of associating asexuality with death, as a way to emphasize the lack of humanity supposedly present in the asexual mind.

A notable example comes from Garth Nix's book, *Clariel*. The titular character Clariel is a necromancer and is also confirmed to be aroace. She is highly misanthropic, and despite the existence of alloromantic and allosexual people who use necromancy, she is the only one who turns truly evil.

Lord Voldemort could also be said to fit this trope—his name roughly translates to "theft from death" because he deals so much in horcruxes and killing. His character is strongly associated with death and is the only character in the series to be asexual (some argue for Charlie, too, but it remains unconfirmed).

It's important to note that the Death-Adjacent Asexual mostly occurs accidentally, as when a character dies, they're portrayed as free from all desires of the flesh, including sex. However, it's still a link to the concept of sexual feelings being a part of life that's required to be a full human.

When you write your characters, feel free to make them whatever orientation you want, but know that it can be harmful to write characters as asexual for the sole purpose of making them seem less human than the other characters. We are just as human as the rest of you, and we'd appreciate being portrayed as such.

Character & Story Implications

Your asexual character may be just as human as the rest of your characters, but your other characters may not necessarily see them that way. Here are a few things to consider in your writing:

Because of the popular trope of the dehumanized asexual and its prevalence in the modern world, other characters might misunderstand your character at a fundamental level. It's possible that some of those characters might even fear your character, seeing them as unnatural and not a good fit for their "normal" lives. If your character also has a cluster B personality disorder, then other characters might end up perceiving them as evil even if that couldn't be further from the truth.

On that note, however, be careful when incorporating cluster B disorders with asexual characters. Often, that is all the thought that goes into creating a stereotypical evil mastermind, and while evil characters can both be asexual and have a cluster B personality disorder, using them as the basis for their evil is both an inaccurate depiction of asexuality and a stigmatizing depiction of real people with those disorders. Besides, it makes for boring writing.

Other characters might actually be familiar with these tropes and believe them in regard to asexual people. Your character may find that they are being given the cold shoulder in several scenarios just because other characters do not understand that what they see on the big screen doesn't translate to real life well.

If your character is actually evil, then consider giving your character more human motivation for their villainy. Asexual people still care about people, ideals, objects, and other things humans care about. An asexual villain with a vendetta against the hero who accidentally killed their best friend in collateral damage is a lot more interesting than an asexual villain who is evil because they're different and different is evil.

If your character is not actually human, and you still want them to discover what it's like to be human, consider utilizing things like platonic love, duty, loss, and sacrifice to humanize them.

Sexual attraction isn't the only thing that makes a human a human, and in the end, they're much more complicated than a single sensation ever will be.

---

1. https://medium.com/dose/no-asexuals-arent-sociopaths-and-robots-349779c750b4
2. https://www.leoconnacht.com/wp/2018/02/in-stillness-the-perception-of-asexuality-in-seanan-mcguires-every-heart-a-doorway/

7

LEGALITY

S ome notes to keep in mind when reading this section:

This entire guide is present-focused and US-centric due to the knowledge bases of those of us who worked on it. This section is particularly focused on the implications of the United States legal system, not because it is the only legal system that impacts asexual people, but the rather the only one on which we can speak. Like other other sexual minorities, asexuals exist across the world, under a wide variety of government and legal frameworks.

Legal advice: we are not lawyers (this guide is offered as writing advice; please contact a professional for any personal legal questions!).

Unfortunately, our invisibility in society at large also means invisibility in terms of legal resources, explainers, and aid. For asexuals trying to figure out the legal implications of our identities on marriage, child custody, medical care, housing, employment, this can pose a barrier.[12] This has tangible impacts on the lives of asexual people. Headlines cover the legal implications of Supreme Court cases on same-sex marriage or trans employment.

Lambda Legal and The Human Rights Council, among other similar organizations, have truly excellent resources depicting the states in which being trans or same-sex attracted is protected in housing, schooling, employment, and marriage. These resources are invaluable, including for some asexuals (who can hold other queer identities along with asexuality!)

No one should need legal training to be able to understand whether they have equal rights. We need equal rights as a community, and we need to be able to easily determine what our rights are.

Visibility is still an important part of activism for our community—on the legal front, so that we are remembered both in advocating for changing laws, and so that we are included when laws are written.[3]

A lot of these legal implications are only relevant for asexuals who do not, or only rarely, have sex. These laws are an asexual issue by virtue of their impact on asexuals due behavior related to our identities. None of this lessens the importance, the validity, or the asexuality of asexuals who do have frequent sex.

Just as many non-discrimination protections don't include sexual orientation, many of the laws that are intended to protect the LGBT+ community are worded in such a way as to exclude asexuality. This may be due to ignorance rather than discriminatory intent, but leaves the asexual community unprotected all the same.[4]

Take the 2020 Supreme Court decision the headlines widely described as a victory for LGBTQ+ rights; while unquestionably a victory, there are questions on the implications for the identities in the +. The decision does not explicitly include other sexualities, but lawyers and journalists were already clarifying the day of the decision that the logic used by the court likely protects other sexualities with a component of same-sex attraction, because in being penalized for same-sex attraction, they are being penalized for something a member of the opposite sex would not be.

But does "an employer who fires an individual merely for being gay or transgender violates Title VII" also mean that an employer who fires someone for being asexual violates Title VII? I certainly don't know—and that same uncertainty was echoed throughout the sexual orientation protections in the US. Some laws and regulations prohibit discrimination based on sexual orientation period; others explicitly discuss orientations that cannot be discriminated against, and leave us out.

The one exception: the State of New York considers us a protected class! So, too, do a handful of municipalities (mostly in New York).[5]

DO ASEXUALS EVEN NEED PROTECTION AGAINST discrimination?

Several studies have found that asexuals face bias at similar or higher rates than other sexual minorities. A 2012 study by Cara C. MacInnis and Gordon Hodson found that people of all sexualities viewed asexuals as significantly less human than homosexuals and bisexuals, who are in turn viewed as less human than heterosexuals. This correlates with a frequent anecdote in asexual discussions: the experience of being told or described as less of a person than others.[678]

Marriage

Annulment: Nonconsummation and impotence (physical or mental) are both grounds for an annulment in an alarming number of US states. For asexuals who do not have sex, both aspects can be troubling. While the word consummation may evoke images of historical romances, it plays a real role in current US (and, as mentioned, that of other countries) law regarding annulment of marriages. [91011]

Annulment has different legal ramifications that divorce; divorce ends an existing marriage, while annulment says that the marriage never existed in the first place.[1213]

Within the asexual community, this is largely viewed as a hypothetical problem—one that could happen, but hasn't happened (enough or at all) within the community for it to exist even as anecdotes. With our level of relative invisibility, anecdata is the closest we can get for issues that haven't or have barely been studied in regards to our community. Until and unless someone this has happened to says so and the story travels, it will remain a hypothetical discussion.

But hypothetical does not mean harmless, and the sheer amount of worrying in forums and chats that it might matter is its own type of cost.

Constructive Desertion

Constructive desertion is when one party "leaves" a marriage without physically leaving. Withholding sex (and isn't there so much to unpack, just in that phrasing?) can be used as justification to hold the withholding party at fault for the divorce. Unlike the above concerns around consummation, there is abounding anecdata about damage caused by this legal framework, and the societal views that back it up.

Immigration and Consummation

Consummation has current implications on the law here, too—and a lot of complications to go with it. A marriage can be valid for immigration purposes without consummation in theory; in practice, consummation or its lack is a factor of consideration in determining whether a marriage was entered into for immigration purposes or in good faith. Proxy marriages (marriages where a couple was married without being in the same physical space at the same time) meanwhile explicitly require proof of consummation.[1415]

The above concerns were about penalties towards marriage; but what about the penalties for not getting married? While the total asexual population is hard to measure, and the studies that have been done are affected by small sample size, the studies that have been done indicate a higher proportion of single people among asexuals.

We are far from the only group affected by the importance our state and society put on one particular form of relationship at the expense of others; many of us (especially aro aces) are, still, affected.[16]

CHARACTER & STORY IMPLICATIONS

How these factors impact a character depend on the location and the time in which the story is taking place, as well as the other identities involved. A nonbinary asexual in a crumbling marriage in present day Wales is going to be a very different story from a an asexual woman in colonial America.

Your character could not be personally affected by any of this, but worry, or technically be affected but not actually have it impact their lives.

Maybe they've never considered any of the above, and then they hear a story of a friend of a friend and suddenly worry about their own situations, or feel angry.

Maybe they are or consider themselves more impacted by the lack of legal protection in their area for their same-gender relationship.

Maybe they're a teenager looking up free legal resources to see if they have protection against their parents putting them on hormones to "fix" their asexuality, and coming up empty.

Maybe they're in immigration proceedings related to marriage, and so the US government's ideas of what constitutes a real marriage are top of mind. Maybe it's traumatic, or an in-joke for them and their spouse, or somewhere in between. The emotional impacts might also be relevant for a character who isn't experiencing this personally, but is affected by outward ripples from someone who is: the character's friend or coworker, the character reading about it in law school, the character whose family member is trying to bring their spouse over, etc.

In closing, some questions that might be useful for settling on the implications for your character are what the relevant laws are in that setting; whether the character is aware of those laws; if they are aware, whether they care; and whether the story focuses on a subject where these laws would be especially salient (discrimination, immigration, divorce).

---

1. https://www.nolo.com/legal-encyclopedia/child-custody-faq.html#answer-1736993
2. https://www.divorcenet.com/resources/divorce/divorce-and-children/the-best-interests-child-factors-a-
3. https://asexualagenda.wordpress.com/2014/09/22/asexuality-may-not-have-direct-legal-issues-and-we-dont-have-to/
4. https://scholarship.law.columbia.edu/cgi/viewcontent.cgi?article=2787&context=faculty_scholarship
   Note that this source conflates asexuality with lack of sex. Citation 351 has a list of municipalities that have added asexuality as a protected class.
5. https://ag.ny.gov/civil-rights/sonda-brochure
6. https://www.huffpost.com/entry/asexual-discrimination_n_3380551?13717+33068=
7. https://www.psychologytoday.com/us/blog/without-prejudice/201209/prejudice-against-group-x-asexuals

8. https://journals.sagepub.com/doi/abs/10.1177/1368430212442419
9. https://www.asexuality.org/en/topic/173936-what-kind-of-legal-right-an-ace-can-be-deprived-of/consummation/
10. https://www.asexuality.org/en/topic/41534-annulment-of-marrige-due-to-non
11. https://www.asexuality.org/en/topic/199132-consummation-laws/?tab=comments#comment-1063845320
12. https://family.findlaw.com/divorce/how-marriage-annulments-differ-from-divorces-and-the-grounds-for.html
13. https://www.legalzoom.com/articles/whats-the-legal-difference-between-annulment-and-divorce
14. https://www.nolo.com/legal-encyclopedia/when-proxy-or-skype-marriages-are-valid-for-green-card-purposes.html
15. https://www.uscis.gov/policy-manual/volume-12-part-g-chapter-2
16. https://www.peerallylaw.com/is-a-marriage-valid-for-immigration-purposes-even-if-not-consummated/

8

WHO'S WHO: VOCABULARY

Before we discuss vocabulary, it's important to understand the Split Attraction Model: what it is, who uses it, and some of the pushback around it. [1]

THE SPLIT ATTRACTION MODEL

This is the concept that romantic and sexual attraction are two separate things, and that one person might feel each differently toward different groups of people. Asexual and aromantic communities widely use this logical framework because it fits with and helps to explain a lot of the experiences of both communities. This framework is useful in considering the other words in this section, and the rest of the guide.

Under this model, a person's full orientation is usually written out with their gender-specific romantic orientation followed by their gender-specific sexual orientation.

For example, a person might be called "homoromantic asexual," or "aromantic pansexual," or "heteroromantic heterosexual," etc. (The exception to this word order pattern is "lesbian," which tends to be listed second both when used to refer to sexual and romantic attraction.)

But ultimately, the order depends on the preferences of the person in question.

It is also possible to have split attraction beyond the asexual and aromantic spectrums; there are panromantic heterosexuals, bi-romantic lesbians, and so forth for whom the Split Attraction Model is very useful to their concept of identity without any aspect of that identity including asexuality or aromanticism.

Some people subscribe to the Split Attraction Model, but prefer to identify themselves primarily by one label (for example, a panromantic asexual might choose to identify themselves as "pan" rather than "pan ace"). This can be due to feeling closer to one community than the other, or feeling more invested in one identity of the other, or feeling that one identity is more relevant for others to know.

It's also possible for people to use different labels in different contexts (in our example above, the individual in question could be closeted to their parents, identify as "pan" at GSA, and identify as "pan-ace" to the people that they date) based on the identity reasons above, or for the sake of the audience—whether it's safe to be out to them one on front but not another, whether they know or might not be familiar with various labels, etc.

Pushback Against the Split Attraction Model

There are some asexuals and aromantics who disagree with the Split Attraction Model, especially aromantic asexuals. Even asexuals and/or aromantics who use Split Attraction Model-based orientation labels can reject the model itself.

That being said, the majority of the pushback against the Split Attraction Model comes from the larger queer community. One argument is the Split Attraction Model sexualizes pre-existing orientations, contributing to societal fetishization of sexual minorities.

Another argument is that the Split Attraction Model waters down the labels. Arguments used against the examples listed above are that a panromantic heterosexual person isn't actually pansexual, and so shouldn't be allowed to use the pan label for themselves, while a biromantic lesbian has some amount of attraction to men and so shouldn't be allowed to use the term lesbian. These arguments tend to be used together, generally as larger patterns of identity gatekeeping.

Because pushback against the Split Attraction Model tends to come from people who are pushing back against asexuals and aromantics in general, there is a connotation of that prejudice in arguments against the Split Attraction Model.

Because of the divided views on it, the Split Attraction Model can be useful in gauging broader views on asexuals and aromantics. Note, too, that even when someone disagrees with the model, they may. choose to use it for safety reasons.

However your character decides to label their sexuality, consider thinking through their reasoning in regards to the Split Attraction Model.

VOCABULARY

Allo: The prefix "allo" is used both to denote someone who is not asexual, and someone who is not aromantic. This means that beyond aromantic asexuals (frequently shortened to "aroaces"), someone can be alloace or alloaro. The more specific terms for each are "allosexual" or "alloromantic," but the shorter term "allo" is much more common.

Graysexuality/Gray-sexuality, Gray-asexuals, and Graces (rarely): Graysexuality or gray-sexuality refers to the gray area on the spectrum between asexual and allosexual. Graysexuality is usually categorized under the asexual umbrella, but some graysexuals prefer "demisexual".

Some common reasons graysexuals identify with the label are: the imagery of an asexual to allosexual spectrum and feel that they are part way along it; feeling that "asexual" fits somewhat, but not entirely; feeling sexual attraction intermittently; and/or feeling ambiguous about sexual attraction as a whole.

Demisexual: Demisexual people ("demis") do not experience sexual attraction without an emotional connection to the person they are attracted to. The term appears to have originated on the Asexual Visibility and Education Network ("AVEN").[2]

A demisexual must first form an emotional connection to a person in order to find that person sexually attractive.

Note that an emotional connection is necessary for but not a guarantee of attraction. (If you took any logic classes, think "necessary but not sufficient condition.")

Some demisexuals consider demisexuality to be a subset of gray-asexuality; others don't, and those that don't can be both demisexual and grayasexual.

A-spec or Aspec: Less commonly used than "aroace", A-spec is an adjective that is short for both "aromantic spectrum" and "asexual spectrum".

Some aromantic asexuals prefer this term because it combines both identities into a single term.

For some aromantic asexuals, this is because both aspects are not two orientations but a single one: they are not aromantic and asexual on separate axis, but rather have a single, cohesive identity that applies to both the sexual and romantic axis. That being said, aro-ace is a much more frequently used term than aspec.

Tension around "Aspec"

There is a sizeble amount of tension around this term. As part of general hate campaigns against the asexual and aromantic communities, members of anti-asexual and anti-trans hate groups have spread the idea that aspec is a term for people with Asbergers and/or people on the autism spectrum, and so was appropriated by the asexual and aromantic communities.

Whether or not the term aspec was actively used by the autistic community before the asexual and aromantic communities, and whether it was actively used by the autistic community at all before that campaign is a matter of ongoing debate. Various internet sleuths have thrown their hats in the ring to evaluate usage, prevalence, and attempt to pinpoint the first time each term was used in reference to each community.

There is also controversy within the autistic community about this, on the grounds that it was never actively used by autistic people to refer to themselves, and so is not a display of allyship but instead an example of allistics imposing themselves on autistic people.

The implications of this debate on current usage is that aspec is rarely, but increasingly (or newly, depending on your sources), used by autistic people to refer to themselves. Some asexuals and aromantics stopped using it to refer to themselves due to this; others, especially some who are also autistic, have deliberately started using it to refer to their sexual and romantic orientations as a push back. Which trend has outweighed the other is, at this point, up to an enterprising statistician to discover.

CHARACTER & STORY IMPLICATIONS

When asexual characters use asexual labels (and when they don't)

Sexuality does not come with a free dictionary (unless it does and mine just got lost in the mail).

How does your character primarily identify? Do they prioritize their sexual or romantic orientation, use both, or view both as secondary to the other facets of their identity?

Societal context is also important to consider. Because asexuality is so invisible in public dialogue, explicitly using words associated with asexuality is important and impactful for asexual people as a whole.

Asexuality often seems to be invisible. Many people who identify as asexual were well into adulthood or even old age before they learned that they fit within the criteria of asexuality. The same is true for gray and demisexuals.

Because it's such a common experience for real people to be unfamiliar with labels or asexuality criteria, creating a character who is not aware of and who doesn't use these terms is a valuable form of representation.

If the story takes place in a historical setting where these labels are anachronistic, consider a) what terms were in use at that time that might not correspond exactly but might apply b) whether there other anachronistic elements to the story, such that this addition makes relatively little difference to the historical accuracy while making a huge difference to the people reading it.

That being said, people who are aware of the term asexual and identify with it will generally be familiar with the other terms. An asexual character who spent months or years figuring out their own identity will very likely know all of these terms. An asexual character is more likely to use these words in dialogue when speaking to another asexual. The amount that they use these words in their thoughts is likely to depend on how often they are using those words out loud in conversation with others.

It is also incredibly valuable to read your own identity on the page. "The Dumbledore Rule" is relevant here—how the character is explicitly identified within the text is what matters for the reader.

With this in mind, I would recommend using the words that the asexual community uses unless there are strong reasons not to. If not knowing that asexuality exists, or that there are others like them, is a key part of the story, then it makes sense to keep these words out of the story—and makes sense to handle the entire subject with care, and a potential explanation for the reader's sake.

---

1. https://www.huffpost.com/entry/asexual-spectrum_n_3428710?1371648467
2. https://www.asexuality.org/

9

COMMON CONFLATIONS

Asexuality is often conflated with other identities, behaviors, and stereotypes, such as aromanticism, low or absent sex drive/libido, aversion to sex, and celibacy. These can all coexist with asexuality, but don't have to — and even the people for whom these do coincide have different preferences on framing the intersections between them.

Some asexuals prefer to include these identities and actions in their own asexual identity. Others view them as separate. For example, there are asexual people for whom not having sex is part and parcel with them being asexual. Other asexual people, including asexual people who do not have sex, believe that asexual is something you are, while sex is something you do. Still others incorporate their personal attitudes into their larger asexual identity: they are not just asexual, but a sex-repulsed/neutral/positive asexual.

Importantly, allosexual (non-asexual) people tend to conflate all of these due to not understanding what asexuality is, which can be upsetting even for the people who do group some of these things into their asexual identity!

Aromanticism

Aromanticism is a lack of romantic attraction. Some people are both (aroace)! The ace and aro communities interact and intersect a lot, but are not identical.

Aversion/Attitudes Towards Having Sex

Sex-repulsion/sex-aversion is the most common asexual attitude towards personal involvement in sex. For many sex-repulsed aces, sex-repulsion is an intrinsic part of their asexuality.

However, not all aces are sex-repulsed. People can be indifferent towards or enjoy sex and still be ace! It's also possible for people's attitudes to fluctuate. One example would be someone who was sex-indifferent for years, but eventually is sex repulsed; another example would be someone who varies between sex positivity and sex indifference from day to day, or month to month.

*   *   *

DISTINCT FROM SOCIOPOLITICAL VIEWS ON SEX

Someone can have political views that sex should be less prevalent in society and media, and be open or enthusiastic to having it themselves. Someone can support sexual openness in larger society, but not be personally interested in having it. While people's personal and societal attitudes towards sex can correspond, they can also be mixed and matched without delegitimizing either.

AVEN has a good chart breaking this down.[1]

*   *   *

SEX DRIVE/LIBIDO

Some asexuals have no sex drive, while others have a typical or high sex drive. Just as this is distinct from asexuality, it's also distinct from sex-repulsion or favorability; people can be asexual, sex-repulsed, and have a high sex drive, or any combination thereof.

Celibacy/Having Sex

Many (possibly most) asexual people choose not to have sex, but some do. Common motivations include emotional intimacy, physical pleasure, wanting to make arousal "go away", or compromise with a partner. And as discussed in the sections on gray-asexuality and demisexuality, not every person on the asexual spectrum feels "100% asexual" at all times, though some do.

Sex as Distinct from Masturbation

Although most asexuals do not have sex with a partner or partners, a far higher proportion do masturbate. Although studies on asexuals and sexual activity are so far small enough to yield statistically different results, the pattern does seem to be that fewer asexuals than allosexuals masturbate, and those that do so less frequently. Those who do tend to describe it differently than allosexuals; common descriptions tend to be that it is useful, fun, done to relieve tension, helps with sleep, or necessary to make arousal go away. That being said, some asexuals do discuss it the same way as allosexuals do.[2]

REPRESSION, FEAR OF SEX

Asexuality is not the same as fear of sex; asexuality is not caused by fear of sex. However, asexuality can factor into fear of rape.

Many asexuals do not want to have sex, and so can fear the prospect of sex with anyone just as a straight woman might fear sex with a woman or a lesbian might fear sex with a man or anyone could fear sex that technically falls within their orientation, but is still unwanted: sex that you don't want to have is rape, and is a frightening prospect. When all sex is unwanted, this can make all sex rape and thus frightening.

While this fear can become a mental health problem if interfering with a person's life, it is important to recognize that even in such instances, that fear of sex is and needs to be approached as fear of rape.

I do want to emphasize again here that while many asexual people do not want to have sex, some do, and they are just as asexual as any other asexual.

Asexuals can also be abuse survivors: just as people of all genders can be sexually assaulted, people of all sexual orientations can be assaulted. Having suffered sexual trauma does not invalidate someone's asexuality. The fact that someone has experienced sexual trauma does not mean that their asexuality needs to be fixed.

In fact, the urge to "fix" asexuality can create sexual trauma: therapists who urge asexual people to have sex and "get better" and significant others who forces sexual contact to "help" their partner are sadly common experiences for asexual people. While nonconsensual sexual activity is never acceptable, professionals and people's support networks can opine that it is, which can create its own level of trauma.

Character & Story Implications

Your asexual character can have any number of sexual and romantic histories, behaviors, and attitudes.

It is one thing for your character to conflate these things together in regards to their own identity; I would avoid having them conflate them in regards to other ace individuals, or asexuals as whole.

---

1. https://www.asexuality.org/?q=attitudes.html
2. https://www.psychologytoday.com/us/blog/living-single/201609/asexuality-is-sexual-orientation-not-sexual-dysfunction

10

SYMBOLS

The asexual community uses several different symbols to identify themselves to others and to fellow asexuals. It's important to familiarize yourself with these symbols, because incorporating them will help create a realer and more believable portrayal of modern asexuality to your audience.

If your character is out of the closet, they will likely use one or more of these symbols. An activist might actively display the ace pride flag, while someone who wants to stay more under the radar might use the black ring. Symbols such as the ace of hearts or the ace of spades are rather niche, however, and will only likely see use if your character is heavily involved in the ace community.

All of these symbols are fairly new and didn't really come into existence until the 21st century, so be aware that if you're writing realistic fiction, your character won't likely have any representation unless the story takes place in the last 10-15 years.

ACE PRIDE FLAG

Perhaps the most recognizable symbol of asexuality is the ace pride flag. It was created in 2010 by AVEN user "standup" during a community effort to establish a flag. It consists of four different-colored stripes that run across the whole flag, with each color holding its own meaning.

The top stripe is black, to represent asexuals and asexuality. The second stripe is gray, to represent demisexuals, gray asexuals, and others who are not fully asexual but fall somewhere on the asexuality spectrum. The third stripe is white, to represent our allosexual allies, those who are not on the asexual spectrum but who support our decisions and don't invalidate our identities or our struggles. Lastly, the bottom stripe is purple, to represent the sense of community that we've developed for ourselves.

This flag is typically the only ace symbol that people will be familiar with, if they're familiar with any.

BLACK RING

Another symbol used by the asexual community to identify each other is a black ring, worn on the right middle finger. The symbol originated on an asexuality.org forum in 2005 when members of the community got together online to determine a way to identify each other without having to give themselves away to others around them.

It is important to note, however, that the ring must be worn on the middle finger in order to be considered an asexual symbol, as wearing the black ring on any other finger on the right hand signifies a member of the swinger community, which is just about the exact opposite of what most asexuals would want to be identified with.

To keep in style with their nicknames, aces will sometimes represent their split-model orientation with either an ace of hearts or an ace of spades. The ace of spades represents an aromantic asexual, or aroace for short, while an ace of hearts represents an alloromantic asexual, sometimes shortened to alloace. Occasionally the ace of diamonds and the ace of clubs are used by others on the ace spectrum, but these do not yet have consistent meanings across ace culture and are not in standard use.

AVEN TRIANGLE

Another symbol to be aware of is the AVEN triangle. Created in 2001, the AVEN triangle is a downward facing triangle with a gradient going from white on top to black on bottom.

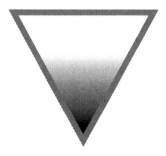

The top line represents the Kinsey scale, a scale used to determine someone's sexuality on a sliding scale from strictly heterosexual to strictly homosexual with bisexuality in the middle. The gray section represents demisexuals, and the very bottom of the triangle is black, to symbolize asexuals and their lack of placement on the scale.

There exists controversy around this symbol, with some claiming that the upside down triangle is an attempt at reclamation from an era when Nazis would mark LGBTQIA+ people with upside down triangles in order to mark them for the camps. This has been stated to be false, and the AVEN triangle has nothing to do with any other triangles others may have claimed. Still, it's good to be aware of the uncertainty behind the symbol.

CAKE

While it isn't so much a symbol as it is a recurring joke within the asexual community, some asexuals will ask joke questions such as "Why have sex when you can have cake/dragons/garlic bread?"

While many asexuals including myself agree that there are things much better than the prospect of sex (my mouth is watering just thinking about garlic bread right now), others can find these jokes offensive and infantilizing. As such, these phrases aren't seeing as much use, and when they are in use, they are almost strictly use by the asexual community.

If you are allosexual, tread lightly when mentioning these jokes in your stories. However, cake in and of itself is still used as an informal asexual symbol and is used to welcome new users to AVEN.

CHARACTER & STORY IMPLICATIONS

The symbols associated with your character could potentially be a source of conflict, especially if your character has run-ins with characters who advocate asexual erasure, whether online or in person. Keep that in mind as you write your character. In addition, consider the following:

Does your character tend to stand their ground when they're confronted with discrimination based on their orientation?

If yes, then they're more likely to display their sexuality via things like the ace pride flag. Typically, those who advertise their sexuality in such a manner are not as intimidated by those who would seek to put them down.

If no, then the only symbol they use might be the ring, as it's mostly known by other asexuals. Your character might not even use symbols if they feel like they could be attacked for it.

Also of note: if your character uses the black ring, then that could create uncomfortable situations if someone approaches them, thinking them to be a swinger, as the distinction is not necessarily very well known.

11

FINAL TAKEAWAYS

While we've referenced "the asexual community" a lot in this Guide, sexual orientation is not an inherently communal identity.

There are asexual people who hang out at ace meetups or in ace chatrooms, participate in asexual penpal programs, intentionally build a network of people who share an identity; there are asexual people who have friends that they the know are also asexual, but care more about the myriad of other things that they have in common; there are asexual people who don't know anyone that (to their knowledge) is also asexual.

Whatever their situation, each is as asexual as the other. They are all asexual.

No individual or organization is the end all be all authority on asexuality, just as there is no final arbitrator on being gay or straight. Try to avoid implying that one asexual character is what all asexual people are like. (One easy way to do this is to have two asexual characters in the story, each with different personalities.)

Important: if your story has a damaging trope, or misunderstands asexuality, that does not make you a bad person or a bad writer. By the same token, just because something is a trope or has fraught connotations doesn't mean you shouldn't write it; it does mean that you should be thoughtful about the implications your writing will have.

This resource is here to give you the tools to rewrite problematic tropes, to help you learn, grow, and be kind in your writing. That includes being kind to yourself.

Thank you for taking the time to learn more about us, and good luck with your writing!

#WRITEDIVERSITYRIGHT PLEDGE

Join us on social media with your #WriteDiversityRight pledge. Tag us in your post—we want to hear from you!

I pledge to do my absolute best, do my due diligence, hire a sensitivity reader(s), and listen to and boost asexual voices.

AFTERWORD

Thank you for reading our Incomplete Guide! We hope you found it helpful. Please leave a review so that other people can find it.

You heard from many of our asexual readers in this book, and you've gotten a taste of what sort of people they are: kind, thoughtful, wise, and really, really cool. And best of all? They love stories.

Check out our wide array of readers at www.saltandsagebooks.com. Tell us that you came through the Incomplete Guide for a 10% discount.

You can find us on Twitter, Instagram, and Facebook—just search "Salt and Sage Books."

If you are an asexual creator and would like to contribute to a future, expanded version, we want to hear from you! Reach out to hello@saltandsagebooks.com and use the subject "INCOMPLETE".

ADDITIONAL RESOURCES: WEBSITES

Here is a list of websites and articles for further education. Remember: none of these websites represent all asexual people and experiences, and that everyone has identities that impact their lives experiences beyond sexual orientation!

Introductory website for asexuality: http://www.whatisasexuality.com, http://wiki.asexuality.org/Main_Page

The asexuality archive: http://www.asexualityarchive.com

Asexual census: https://asexualcensus.wordpress.com. Small enough not to reflect the whole asexual population, but a useful resource for looking at intersections of experiences and identities.

AVEN: https://www.asexuality.org. The best known asexuality resource.

More on Aromantics: https://aromantic.wikia.org/wiki/Aromantics_Wiki

More on Demisexuality: https://demisexuality.org/articles/what-is-demisexuality/

https://www.wired.com/2015/02/demisexuality/

More on Graysexuality: https://demisexuality.org/articles/what-is-gray-asexuality/

Teen Vogue also has a lot of good articles on asexuality:

https://www.teenvogue.com/story/what-asexuality-means

https://www.teenvogue.com/story/being-asexual-is-totally-fine

https://www.teenvogue.com/story/how-to-know-if-youre-asexual-or-just-not-ready-to-have-sex

Books Featuring Asexual Characters

These are just a few book suggestions—Google is your friend, and so is The Aromatic and Asexual Character's Database[1]!

Afterworlds by Scott Westerfeld

Banner of the Damned by Sherwood Smith

Before I Let Go by Marieke Nijkamp

Belle Revolte by Linsey Miller

Beneath the Citadel by Destiny Soria

Beyond the Black Door by AdriAnne Strickland

Black Wings Beating by Alex London

Carrie Pilby by Caren Lissner

City of Strife by Claudie Arsenault

The Cybernetic Tea Shop by Meredith Katz

Dare Mighty Things by Heather Kaczynski

Deadly Sweet Lies by Erica Cameron

Demonosity by Amanda Ashby

Dread Nation by Justina Ireland

The Faerie Godmother's Apprentice Wore Green by Nicky Kyle

Fire's Stone by Tanya Huff

Gods, Monsters, and the Lucky Peach by Kelly Robson

This Golden Flame by Emily Victoria

Guardian of the Dead by Karen Healey

Hullmetal Girls by Emily Skrutskie

The Lady's Guide to Petticoats and Piracy by Mackenzi Lee

Let's Talk About Love by Claire Kann

Luna New Moon by Ian McDonald

Lunaside by J. L. Douglas

The Mystic Marriage by Heather Rose Jones

Not Your Backup by C. B. Lee

The Perfect Assassin by K. A. Doore

Quicksilver by R.J. Anderson

Secondhand Origin Stories by Lee Blauersouth

Sinners by Eka Waterfield

The Spy with the Red Balloon by Katherine Locke

Tarnished are the Stars by Rosiee Thor

Tash Hearts Tolstoy by Kathryn Ormsbee

Vengeful by V. E. Schwab

Winter Tide by Ruthanna Emrys

---

1. http://claudiearseneault.com/?page_id=1320

ABOUT THE AUTHOR

Salt and Sage Books is an editing company centered on the idea that a rising tide lifts all boats.

We are a creative community of devoted readers, writers, and editors, hailing from the desert's sunwashed sage to the coast's shining seas, and we've brought together our diverse skills and experiences in a single welcoming place, to help writers like you.

When you choose Salt and Sage, you join a creative community working together to change the world through story.

Check out our Incomplete Guides series for an accessible first step into writing diversely.

You'll find a wide range of editors, sensitivity and expert readers, and beta readers on our website, www.saltandsagebooks.com.

Welcome to the rising tide.

Writing Queer Characters

Writing Characters from the U.K.

Writing Characters from Spain

Writing about Anxiety

Writing about PTSD and Trauma

Writing about Therapy

And more!

If you'd like to see one of these guides sooner than another or have ideas for another guide, please email us at hello@saltandsagebooks.com.

Made in the USA
Columbia, SC
24 May 2021